O9-ABI-916

ALENA LOMASON MEMORIAL LIBRARY

DISCARD

NUCLEAR ACCIDENT

DISCARD

NUCLEAR ACCIDENT

CHRISTOPHER LAMPTON

THE MILLBROOK PRESS
BROOKFIELD, CT
A DISASTER! BOOK

Photos courtesy of Sovfoto: cover, pp. 6, 24; U.S. Department
of Energy: pp. 10, 20, 41, 42–43; Smithsonian Institution: p. 14;
Bettmann: pp. 17, 32–33; AP/Wide World: pp. 27, 30; Photo
Researchers: p. 36 (© Joseph Nettis). Illustrations by Pat Scully.

Library of Congress Cataloging-in-Publication Data

Lampton, Christopher.
Nuclear accident / Christopher Lampton.
p.   cm.—(A Disaster! book)
Includes bibliographical references and index.

Summary: Discusses nuclear energy, its source, how it works,
and, giving the examples of Three Mile Island and Chernobyl,
how dangerous it can be when things go wrong.
ISBN 1-56294-073-2 (lib. bdg.)
1. Nuclear power plants—Accidents—Juvenile literature.
[1. Nuclear power plants—Accidents.] I. Title. II. Series:
Lampton, Christopher. Disaster! book.
TK1078.L35   1992
363.17'99—dc20   91-43564   CIP   AC

Copyright © 1992 by Christopher Lampton
All rights reserved
Printed in the United States of America
5   4   3   2   1

CONTENTS

This picture of the Chernobyl nuclear plant clearly shows the damage done by the melt-down of the reactor in 1986.

A REAL
NUCLEAR
DISASTER

Inside the nuclear power plant at Chernobyl, in the Soviet Union, something was very wrong.

A power plant produces *electricity*. At a nuclear power plant, electricity is produced by tapping the energy in the tiny particles called *atoms*. But on April 25, 1986, the engineers and technicians at the Chernobyl power plant began a dangerous experiment.

The result of their experiment was disaster. Deep inside the heart of the power plant, in the part known as the *reactor*, it became very hot. It became so hot, in fact, that the reactor began to melt. Water inside the reactor exploded into steam. The roof blew off the top of the power plant. Hot materials flew through the air.

Many of these hot materials were *radioactive*. We'll explain later what that means. These radioactive materials were so dangerous that just being near them could cause a person to die. But fire-fighters nonetheless worked bravely through the night to put out the fire that raged inside the Chernobyl power plant. Many of them later died—not because of the fire but because of their exposure to these radioactive materials. At least several hundred other people—perhaps as many as 5,000—will eventually die because they were near the Chernobyl plant that night.

Some of the radioactive materials were spread by the wind and by nearby rivers. They were later detected many hundreds and even thousands of miles away. These radioactive materials may eventually cause the deaths of thousands of people around the world.

What happened at Chernobyl was a disaster indeed! To understand this disaster, we'll need to understand some things about nuclear power plants. And to understand nuclear power plants, we'll need to understand a most important concept: energy!

ENERGY AND HOW IT WORKS

Energy is what makes things go. Cars move because they have energy. Baseballs fly through the air because they have energy. Rain falls because it has energy.

But where do these things get their energy? Some things get energy from fuel. The gas that you pump into an automobile, for instance, gives the car the energy that makes it go. The appliances that we have around the house get their energy from electricity. The food that you put into your body gives you the energy that makes *you* go.

Where does the electricity in your home come from? Usually, it is produced in large power plants. Power plants, in turn, need a way to produce electricity. Usually, they produce it by using a special motor called an *electric generator.* But electric generators also need energy to make them go.

There are several ways to produce the energy to operate an electric generator. Fast-flowing water in large rivers, for instance,

At the Chief Joseph Dam, on the Columbia River in Washington State, electricity is generated by water power.

can be used to turn generators and produce electricity. This form of energy production is called *hydropower.*

Or generators can be powered by the light of the sun, shining on special energy-producing devices called *photovoltaic cells.* This form of energy is called *solar power.*

In some power plants, generators are run by burning oil or natural gas. These substances are found deep beneath the ground and pumped to the surface.

However, the most common method of running an electrical generator is to burn coal. Coal is usually found in mines deep inside the earth. Burning coal can be used to boil water, which turns into steam. The force of the rising steam can be used to turn an electric generator.

More than half of the electricity in the United States is produced by burning coal. Coal, oil, and natural gas are types of *fossil fuels.* Fossil fuels were created over millions of years from the remains of once-living organisms. There are drawbacks to using fossil fuels to produce electricity. One of these is that fossil fuels are a *nonrenewable resource.* It takes millions of years and very special conditions for new coal beds to form, for instance. This means that there's a limited supply, and at current rates of usage the coal will run out in less than five hundred years. Another problem with fossil fuels is that they pollute the atmosphere.

What can we do instead of burning fossil fuels to produce electricity? As we saw, there are several other ways to produce large amounts of electricity. But none of those mentioned can yet be used to produce cheaply enough the large amount of electricity that is needed in a country like the United States.

However, there is another method that can be used for large-scale inexpensive energy production. This is called *nuclear energy.*

ENERGY FROM THE ATOM

Everything in the world is made up of atoms. An atom is a unit of matter so tiny that it can't even be seen through a conventional microscope. Even a tiny grain of dust is made up of so many atoms that you would never be able to count them all—even if you could see them.

An object such as this book is made up of far more atoms than is a grain of dust. These atoms are held together by powerful forces, which is why this book doesn't just crumble into a pile of atoms when you pick it up. Nonetheless, you could probably tear this book to pieces. If you did, you would be tearing the atoms in the book apart from one another. However, you would not be dividing the atoms themselves.

Ordinarily, there is no way to break apart an individual atom. In fact, the very word "atom" comes from an ancient Greek word that means "indivisible." Atoms were given this name because it was believed that they could never be split apart. And yet, atoms are made up of even smaller particles. These particles are called *electrons, neutrons,* and *protons.*

If an atom is made up of smaller particles, why can't it be split apart? Because the forces that hold electrons, neutrons, and protons together inside an atom are very powerful.

Still, it *is* possible to split an atom, although scientists didn't know how to do it until a little more than 50 years ago. The easiest atoms to split are very big atoms. When a big atom falls apart,

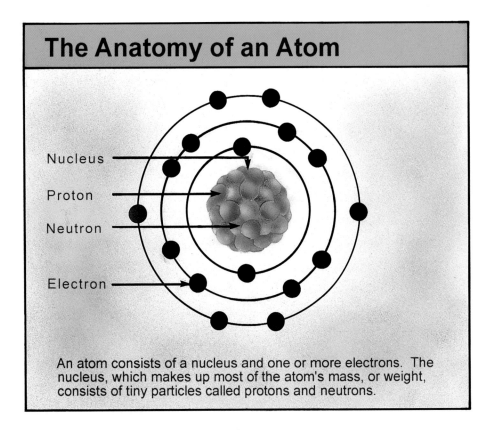

The Anatomy of an Atom

Nucleus

Proton

Neutron

Electron

An atom consists of a nucleus and one or more electrons. The nucleus, which makes up most of the atom's mass, or weight, consists of tiny particles called protons and neutrons.

some of the particles that make up that atom may come shooting out of it, like high-speed bullets. These particles may then hit other atoms and knock them apart, too. Thus, when one atom falls apart, other atoms close to it tend to come apart as well. To use the scientific term, the atoms undergo *fission;* that is, they break apart into smaller atoms.

Take a lot of large atoms, such as the atoms that make up the substances known as *uranium* and *plutonium,* and put them together. They'll start knocking each other apart. In fact, if you throw together large enough amounts of these substances quickly enough, they'll actually explode! (This is the secret behind the atomic bomb. Put the atoms together more slowly, and they'll simply produce a lot of heat.)

Heat is exactly what we need to produce if we want to run an electric generator. And the heat produced by splitting atoms can drive a steam engine and run an electric generator. This is how a nuclear power plant works.

There are problems, however, with this method of generating electricity. The biggest problem is that, when an atom undergoes fission, it produces more than just heat.

Testing an atomic bomb in Nevada. In atomic (or fission) weapons, tremendous destructive force is released when the cores, or nuclei, of certain atoms split.

DANGER: RADIOACTIVITY!

We saw that a splitting atom can cause high-speed particles to be spit out much like bullets from a gun. This burst is referred to as *radioactivity.*

What would happen if you were standing in the way of one of these tiny radioactive bullets when it shot out of an atom? You wouldn't notice it. It would be too small for you to see or feel. But that doesn't mean that it couldn't damage your body.

Radioactivity can damage the body's *cells,* especially dividing cells. Chances are that if one of these tiny, high-speed bullets shoots through your body, it won't cause serious damage. And even if it does, the cells in your body have ways to repair the damage. But if enough of these high-speed particles shoot through your body all at once, they can overwhelm the repair mechanisms in the cells. When this happens, the cells may die immediately, or over a period of time they may start growing in unusual ways. When cells grow

Children in Poland swallow an anti-radiation iodine solution to help prevent radiation sickness after the Chernobyl fallout.

without regard to other cells around them, they can cause a disease called *cancer.*

Radioactivity is dangerous in large amounts. But how much radioactivity is a large amount? The total amount of radioactivity that actually passes through your body is measured with a special unit called the *rem.* Since the rem represents a lot of radioactivity, the *mrem* (short for "millirem," or one one-thousandth of a rem) is often used to measure the smaller amounts of body radioactivity.

A few mrems of radioactivity probably won't hurt you. In fact, your body absorbs about 4 mrems of radioactivity *every week!* (An average X ray contains about 45 to 75 mrems.) Some of the radioactivity in our atmosphere comes from outer space, in what are known as *cosmic rays.*

Exposure to very low levels of radioactivity probably isn't dangerous for human beings. (No one is really sure about what dosage *is* safe.) However, exposure to several rems of radiation is definitely dangerous. This exposure probably won't kill you right away, but it may cause your body to develop cancer years or decades in the future. Exposure to more than about 50 rems may cause radiation sickness, which kills within a few days. And exposure to 1,000 or more rems is always fatal, sometimes within hours.

Nuclear power plants use radioactive substances to run their electric generators. If these substances were ever released into the open air, they would cause terrible problems indeed. That is why the people who build and run nuclear power plants take special precautions to make sure that this never happens.

But sometimes it does anyway.

WHEN
THINGS
GO WRONG

Let's take a look at a typical nuclear power plant to see how it works—and what can go wrong.

As we said earlier, the part of a nuclear power plant that produces electricity from radioactive materials is called the nuclear reactor. The reactor is almost always surrounded by a thick shell of concrete known as the *containment building.* The containment building is designed to "contain" the radioactive materials, so that they can't get out into the surrounding world. The concrete shell of the containment building is so thick that neither an earthquake nor an airplane crash can crack it open!

Uranium and plutonium are both used as fuel in nuclear power plants. They are radioactive substances. When enough uranium or plutonium fuel is placed inside the reactor's *core,* or center, the atoms will start splitting in large numbers. The splitting atoms produce heat. Water is pumped through pipes buried in the fuel in the reactor core. The heat of the fuel causes the water to boil. The steam from the boiling water then runs an electric generator.

A nuclear reactor wouldn't be very useful if there weren't some way to turn it on and off. This is done with the help of *control rods.* These are rods made out of absorbent materials that are *not* radioactive. The fuel in the reactor core contains holes into which these rods can be inserted. With the aid of a machine, the control rods are inserted into these holes to turn off the reactor. The control rods absorb some of the tiny high-speed particles that cause the atoms

A nuclear reactor core at a U.S. Department of Energy test site. When cooled by water, the core has a blue glow.

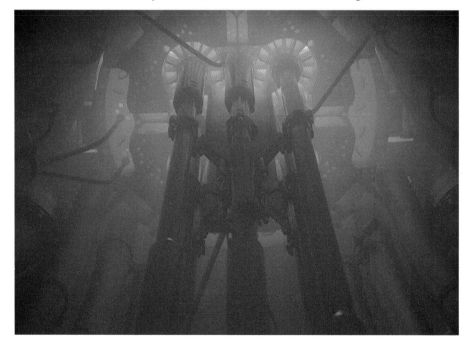

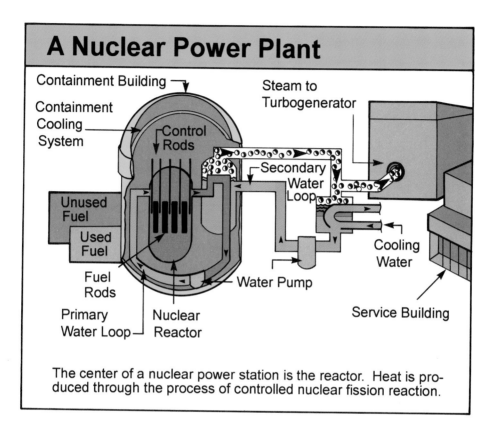

A Nuclear Power Plant

Containment Building

Containment
Cooling
System

Control
Rods

Steam to
Turbogenerator

Secondary
Water
Loop

Unused
Fuel

Used
Fuel

Fuel
Rods

Water Pump

Cooling
Water

Primary
Water Loop

Nuclear
Reactor

Service Building

The center of a nuclear power station is the reactor. Heat is produced through the process of controlled nuclear fission reaction.

in the nuclear fuel to split. When the control rods are in place, the reactor cools down. If the control rods are removed, the reactor heats back up.

If the reactor core is really hot, however, the control rods can't cool it off very quickly. Fortunately, the water that runs through the core to create steam also cools the core.

The worst thing that can happen inside a nuclear reactor is for the water to stop flowing. If it does, the reactor core will be unable to cool down.

Once the water is gone from inside the reactor, the fuel itself will start to melt! And if the fuel melts, the entire reactor core will melt. The molten reactor core can become so hot, in fact, that it can melt its way through the floor of the containment building and at least 15 to 20 feet (4.5 to 6m) into the ground. This kind of nuclear accident is called a *meltdown.*

The molten reactor core is full of radioactive materials, and these materials could contaminate, or poison, the water that runs through the ground. This contaminated water could then travel for long distances, spreading radioactivity far and wide. And if the radioactive water were to spill into a river, it could be carried for hundreds or even thousands of miles.

Worse, the melting reactor core could cause a steam explosion! This isn't the same as a nuclear explosion. But a steam explosion could be powerful enough to do what earthquakes and crashing airplanes cannot. It could break open the top of the containment building and fling radioactive materials into the air! If the wind were blowing strongly enough, these radioactive materials could be carried for many miles.

Before you start worrying that something like this will happen at a nuclear power plant near you, you should know that an accident such as this isn't very likely to happen. As we will see, nuclear power plants are designed so that major accidents very rarely occur. Yet, something very much like this did happen at the nuclear power plant in Chernobyl!

RETURN TO
CHERNOBYL

Now that we know a little about how nuclear power plants work, let's take another look at the 1986 accident at Chernobyl.

The accident would probably never have happened if the engineers who were running the plant hadn't been performing unusual tests. What kinds of tests? They were trying to learn what would happen to a nuclear reactor if all power were lost to the reactor core. If the power were lost, many of the safety systems in the reactor core would cease to function.

Inside the reactor at Chernobyl were a number of large, fan-like devices that spun rapidly while the reactor was running. Such devices are called *turbines.* If the power were to fail inside the reactor, these turbines would continue spinning for some time, just as bicycle wheels keep spinning for a while after you stop pedaling. The idea of the experiment was to see how long the turbines would continue to operate during a power failure.

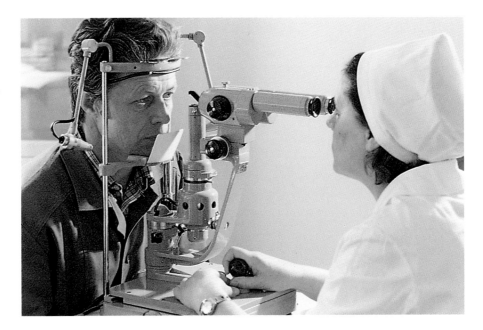

A worker at the Chernobyl plant is given a medical examination.

To perform this experiment, however, it was necessary to simulate a power failure inside the reactor. If the safety devices had been left on, this experiment wouldn't necessarily have been *too* dangerous. But plant authorities turned off the safety devices during the experiment so that they wouldn't affect the results.

For a very brief time, the experiment seemed to be going well. But deep inside the reactor, strange things were happening. The reactor core was growing hotter. Dangerous gases were being produced. By the time the experimenters realized that things were going wrong, it was too late to stop the experiment.

At 1:23 in the morning, the nuclear reactor at Chernobyl exploded. The roof blew off of the reactor building, flinging 50 tons of radioactive fuel into the night sky. Remember, this was a gas explosion, not a nuclear explosion. Nonetheless, one authority has estimated that it was as powerful as ten bombs the size of the atom bomb dropped on the city of Hiroshima, Japan, in 1945.

After the explosion, fires erupted throughout the building and the surrounding area. Firefighters arrived to battle the flames, and they were immediately exposed to the intense radioactivity that had been released by the explosion. By morning, many of them had darkened or even blackened skin, a condition that is referred to as a "nuclear tan."

Many other people nearby were exposed to the radioactivity as well. A pair of fishermen in the nearby waters, for instance, watched the fire burn into the night, without realizing that they were being exposed to a deadly onslaught of invisible particles. Two people died that night during the explosion and the fire that followed. Twenty-nine more would die of radiation poisoning in the weeks ahead.

The wind carried radioactive materials for great distances. The accident took place on a Friday. By the following Monday, radiation was detected in Sweden—on the shoes of a man *entering* the nuclear power plant where he worked. Special detectors elsewhere in that country began to record radioactivity levels 100 times higher than normal. Apparently a cloud of radioactive material had passed over Sweden the previous day. By tracing the path of this cloud backward, Western observers determined that the accident had taken place at Chernobyl.

The levels of radioactivity in Sweden were not immediately dangerous. However, on its way to Sweden, the cloud had passed through several other countries closer to Chernobyl. Radioactivity

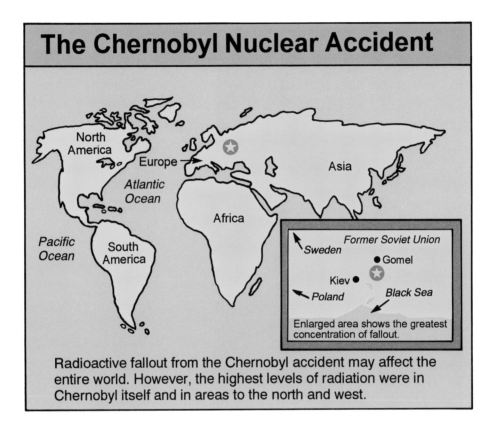

The Chernobyl Nuclear Accident

North America

Europe

Atlantic Ocean

Asia

Africa

Pacific Ocean

South America

Sweden

Former Soviet Union

● Gomel

Kiev ●

Poland

Black Sea

Enlarged area shows the greatest concentration of fallout.

Radioactive fallout from the Chernobyl accident may affect the entire world. However, the highest levels of radiation were in Chernobyl itself and in areas to the north and west.

levels in these countries were higher and are expected to result in thousands of cases of cancer over the next few decades. Further, radioactive substances were discovered in certain foods produced in those countries, including the milk of cows. Eating these foods further increased the radiation exposure of people living in those countries.

Eventually, increased radiation levels were detected in Europe and as far away as the United States. Fortunately, these levels were barely higher than the normal, so few—if any—cases of cancer should occur in these areas due to the Chernobyl incident.

In the aftermath of the Chernobyl explosion,
a German vegetable seller holds up a sign that
reads, "The atoms have destroyed us." Radioactive fallout from the nuclear accident spread
over a wide area, contaminating farm products.

FORTY YEARS OF NUCLEAR ACCIDENTS

The accident at Chernobyl was the worst in the history of nuclear power. However, there have been other accidents at nuclear plants. But fortunately, the safety systems that are intended to prevent large-scale nuclear disasters have done their job very well. On some occasions, however, the people who run the plants haven't done their jobs nearly as well as these safety systems have.

Here are some of the near-disasters that have occurred at nuclear power plants in the last 40 years:

■ During routine maintenance in 1957, some of the pellets of uranium fuel in the Windscale nuclear reactor in England burst open. The uranium inside caught fire. Radioactive fumes began drifting up the plant smokestack into the air outside. The people who operated the plant thought the cooling system had failed and began to fan the flames, only making things worse. So men wearing bulky radiation suits to protect them from the radioactivity entered the reactor core to remove the burning fuel. But the fuel pellets were half melted. They were stuck in place and couldn't be removed. The operators knew that they had to stop the fuel from burning. The only solution was to douse the hot reactor core with large amounts of water, which might actually cause a deadly hydrogen explosion! Finally, more than four days after the incident began, water hoses were turned on the nuclear fuel. Steam shot up the smokestack, but there was no explosion. Unusual amounts of radioactive materials were found in the nearby village, however.

■ In the Soviet Union, a nuclear fuel dump containing used radioactive fuel started producing heat in 1957. A large area around the dump had become contaminated with radioactive materials. The area was evacuated (emptied of people) for many years afterward.

■ A reactor in California suffered a partial meltdown in 1959. This was the first such accident recorded in the United States.

■ A steam explosion killed three people at a reactor in Idaho Falls, Idaho, in 1961.

■ In 1966 the core of the Enrico Fermi nuclear reactor, outside Detroit, Michigan, began to melt. This was caused by a piece of metal that had become jammed in one of the pipes through which cooling liquid normally flowed. Engineers worked desperately for several days to restore the liquid to the core and remove the melted portion of the fuel. The piece of metal turned out to be part of a safety device that had broken off and fallen into the pipes.

■ Thousands of gallons of radioactive water were accidentally dumped into the Mississippi River in 1971 in Minnesota.

■ The core of a reactor in Leningrad, in the USSR, partially melted down in 1975, releasing radioactive materials outside the plant.

The Indian Point nuclear power plant, near New York City, leaked radioactive water in 1985.

■ In 1982 steam from radioactive water sprayed out of a nuclear power plant near Rochester, New York.

■ Radioactive water leaked out of the Indian Point nuclear power plant, outside of New York City, in 1985.

Next to Chernobyl, though, the most publicized nuclear disaster of all time took place a few miles away from Harrisburg, Pennsylvania. To this day, the name of the location of that plant automatically makes one think of nuclear disasters: Three Mile Island.

THREE MILE ISLAND

The accident at the Three Mile Island nuclear power plant began on the morning of March 18, 1979. At that time, a water pump that sent water into the reactor core stopped working.

Fortunately, the Three Mile Island plant was designed to handle accidents like this. It contained additional pumps in case one stopped working.

And yet, within a few hours, the core of the Three Mile Island plant began to melt. Why? Because the failure of the water pump was only the first of several mishaps that occurred that morning. Most of these mishaps were caused by the people who worked at the plant.

For one thing, several valves in the pipes leading to the core had been accidentally left closed a few days before. When the emergency water pumps were turned on, these valves blocked the water. Some water was still able to make its way into the core. But then another valve inside the core became stuck *open,* and the water simply leaked out through the open valve!

As a result, the reactor core almost dried out completely. Alarms went off in the plant's control center, where technicians operated the reactor with the aid of thousands of switches, dials, and gauges.

When the alarms sounded, these technicians immediately tried to figure out what was wrong. Hundreds of red lights flashed on and off in the control center to indicate what the problem was. So many red lights were flashing, in fact, that the technicians became confused. And one of the most important red lights—the one that would have told them that the emergency valves were closed—was covered up by a piece of paper!

The Three Mile Island nuclear reactor near Harrisburg, Pennsylvania, came very close to a major nuclear disaster in 1979 when part of its core melted.

Because they weren't sure what was happening, the plant technicians believed that there was more than enough water in the core. And so they did the worst thing that they could possibly have done. They shut off what little water was actually reaching the core!

At this point, the core of the Three Mile Island reactor began to melt. Fortunately, after two-and-a-half long hours, the technicians finally closed the valve that was letting the water leak out of the core. An hour later, they turned the water pumps back on. As a result, the reactor core melted only partially. It didn't burn its way through the containment building.

Radioactive water poured out of the reactor during the incident into special waste-storage tanks placed near the core. Eventually, these tanks overflowed. A small amount of radioactive material was released into the air outside of the containment building. However, only about 5 mrems of radioactivity were released, which shouldn't have been enough to hurt anyone.

Three Mile Island was not exactly a disaster, because nobody was hurt. But it was a scary reminder of what can go wrong at nuclear power plants.

PREVENTING
NUCLEAR DISASTERS

The easiest way to prevent nuclear power disasters would be to eliminate all nuclear power plants. But it isn't really that simple. Human beings will always need electricity, unless we decide to go back to living in caves. Therefore, we need a way to create that electricity. Nuclear power is one of the best ways that we have.

Nonetheless, people in the United States are reluctant to build new nuclear power plants. In fact, none has been authorized in the United States since the Three Mile Island incident in 1979.

But even if no new nuclear power plants are built, how do we prevent accidents in the ones that already exist? According to most nuclear engineers, the secret to preventing nuclear disasters is *redundancy*. This means that, for every system that can fail in a nuclear power plant, there should be one or more backup systems that can take over in its place. For instance, when a pump fails, there should be another pump ready to do the same job.

To help prevent human error, engineers train in a mock-up
of a nuclear control room in Limerick, Pennsylvania.

But we saw in the description of the Three Mile Island incident that even redundancy doesn't always prevent accidents. When the pump failed in the Three Mile Island core, the backup pump should have taken over. It didn't. The cause of its failure to do so was human error. The people who ran the plant made a mistake—a mistake that nearly led to a complete meltdown. Human error was also the cause of the accident at the Chernobyl reactor. The people who ran the reactor performed dangerous experiments.

So the best method of preventing nuclear power disasters may be to better educate the people who run the nuclear power plants. The more these technicians and engineers know about preventing nuclear disaster, the less likely they are to make the kinds of mistakes that were made at Three Mile Island and Chernobyl. And, in fact, the nuclear power industry in the United States now provides better training programs for its technicians than it did before the Three Mile Island accident. In the Soviet Union, the Chernobyl disaster created a similar awareness of nuclear power dangers.

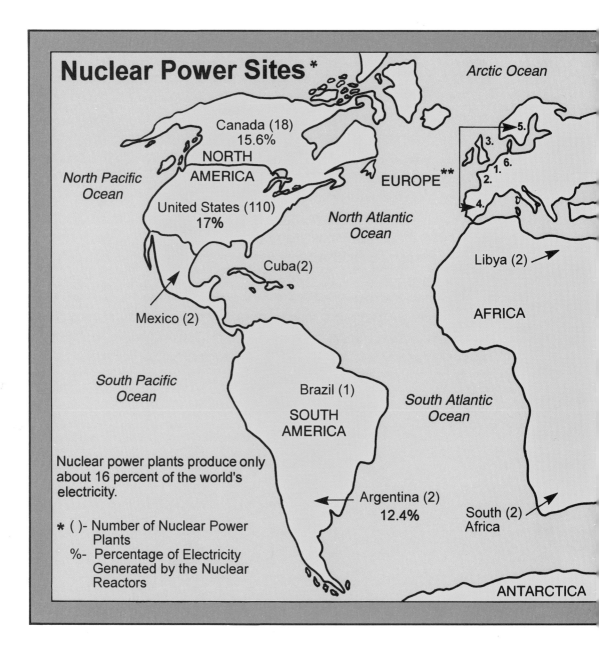

Nuclear Power Sites *

Arctic Ocean

Canada (18)
15.6%

NORTH AMERICA

North Pacific Ocean

United States (110)
17%

EUROPE **

3.
5.
1. 6.
2.
4.

North Atlantic Ocean

Cuba(2)

Mexico (2)

Libya (2)

AFRICA

South Pacific Ocean

Brazil (1)

SOUTH AMERICA

South Atlantic Ocean

Nuclear power plants produce only about 16 percent of the world's electricity.

* ( )- Number of Nuclear Power Plants
%- Percentage of Electricity Generated by the Nuclear Reactors

Argentina (2)
12.4%

South (2)
Africa

ANTARCTICA

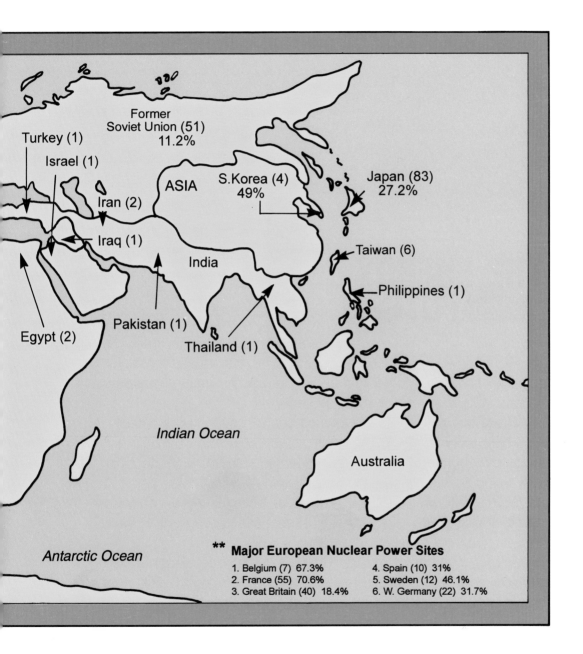

Former
Soviet Union (51)
11.2%

Turkey (1)

Israel (1)

Iran (2)

ASIA

S.Korea (4)
49%

Japan (83)
27.2%

Iraq (1)

India

Taiwan (6)

Philippines (1)

Pakistan (1)

Thailand (1)

Egypt (2)

Indian Ocean

Australia

Antarctic Ocean

** **Major European Nuclear Power Sites**

1. Belgium (7) 67.3%   4. Spain (10) 31%
2. France (55) 70.6%   5. Sweden (12) 46.1%
3. Great Britain (40) 18.4% 6. W. Germany (22) 31.7%

THE ENERGY FUTURE

Eventually, even nuclear fuels will run out. What will we do for electricity then? Are there existing, safer methods of creating electricity that can be used for many thousands of years without our running out of fuel?

There are many alternative methods of generating electricity. We looked at some of them earlier in this book. And scientists are always developing new ones. For instance, we can generate electricity using windmills, just as we generate electricity using dams in the middle of flowing streams. And solar energy may be a major source of electricity in the future. But most alternative methods are still too expensive to be used on a large scale.

In fact, if we want to stop relying on methods of generating electricity that cause pollution or that can result in tragic accidents, we will have to stop using so much electricity. Industry must learn to use electricity more efficiently. Architects need to design homes

As an alternative to nuclear power, solar energy
may be the way of the future. This picture shows
an experimental solar energy plant in California.

that can be heated and lit naturally by the sun. You can even help achieve this goal of energy efficiency yourself, by turning off lights and appliances that are not in use.

We will always need *some* electricity, though. In the future, scientists believe that we will make most of our electricity by using *fusion.* Like today's nuclear power, fusion taps into the power inside the atom. But instead of splitting large atoms apart into smaller atoms (fission), fusion puts smaller atoms together into larger atoms. This releases the same force that makes the sun burn and the stars shine. Fusion is a powerful source of energy indeed!

An experimental fusion reactor, called a tokamak. With devices like this, scientists are seeking ways to produce usable energy through nuclear fusion.

Fusion power doesn't produce radioactivity the way that nuclear reactors do. And a fusion plant could use water for fuel. Since water is one of the most common substances on earth, it would be a long time before a fusion plant would run out of fuel.

Unfortunately, scientists have not yet been able to produce energy economically using fusion. However, they believe that they will someday be able to do it. By the middle of the next century, fusion plants may be ready and waiting to manufacture as much electricity as we need. And then we'll never need to worry again about the dangers of nuclear fission.

GLOSSARY

atoms—the extremely tiny particles that make up all matter on earth.

cancer—a disease that occurs when cells grow in an uncontrollable fashion; sometimes caused by radioactivity.

cells—the tiny compartments that are the building blocks of living organisms.

containment building—the hard "shell" surrounding a nuclear reactor that prevents radioactive materials from reaching the outside world.

control rods—rods made out of nonradioactive materials; used to control the production of heat in a nuclear reactor.

core—the part of a nuclear reactor that contains the nuclear fuel.

cosmic rays—particles of radioactivity from outer space.

electric generator—a machine for creating electricity.

electricity—a form of energy that can travel over long distances in wires.

electron—one of the tiny particles that make up atoms.

fission—the splitting of one large, unstable atom into two or more smaller atoms, releasing energy in the process.

fossil fuels—fuels such as coal, oil, and natural gas.

fusion—a method of generating electricity and other forms of energy using the energy in the center of the atom.

hydropower—a form of energy production that uses moving water to turn electric generators.

meltdown—a nuclear accident in which the reactor core melts from its own heat; usually caused by a loss-of-coolant accident.

mrem—one thousandth of a rem.

neutron—one of the tiny particles that make up atoms.

nonrenewable resource—a natural resource, such as coal, that is available only in limited supply.

nuclear energy—the use of radioactive materials to create electricity.

photovoltaic cells—devices for turning the energy of sunlight into electricity.

plutonium—a radioactive substance that can be used as nuclear fuel.

proton—one of the tiny particles that make up atoms.

radioactive—describes a substance that emits tiny particles that can damage living cells.

radioactivity—the tiny but dangerous particles that shoot out of radioactive substances, such as uranium and plutonium.

reactor—the part of a nuclear power plant that produces electricity from radioactive materials.

redundancy—the use of backup parts to reduce the possibility that a nuclear reactor will fail to work properly.

rem—a unit used to measure the amount of radioactivity absorbed by the human body.

solar power—the creation of electricity and other forms of energy using sunlight.

turbine—a giant fan that spins rapidly in the core of some reactors.

uranium—a radioactive substance that can be used as nuclear fuel.

RECOMMENDED READING

Adler, Irving. *Atomic Energy.* New York: The John Daly Co., 1971.

Coble, Charles. *Nuclear Energy.* Milwaukee: Raintree Publishers, 1973.

Haines, Gail Kay. *The Great Nuclear Power Debate.* New York: Dodd, Mead and Co., 1985.

Halacy, Dan. *Nuclear Energy.* New York: Franklin Watts, 1984.

McKie, Robin. *Nuclear Power.* New York: Gloucester Press, 1985.

Rothman, Milton. *Energy and the Future.* New York: Franklin Watts, 1975.

INDEX